My Alphabet Book

By

Barbara Serling

Illustrated by Joshua Allen

Contents

Mm

Nn

Oo

Pp

Qq

Rr

Ss

Tt

Uu

Vv

Ww

Xx

Yy

Zy

dedicated to Giovanna, Isabella and Jade

<u>Aa</u>

ant

book

cat

dog

eye

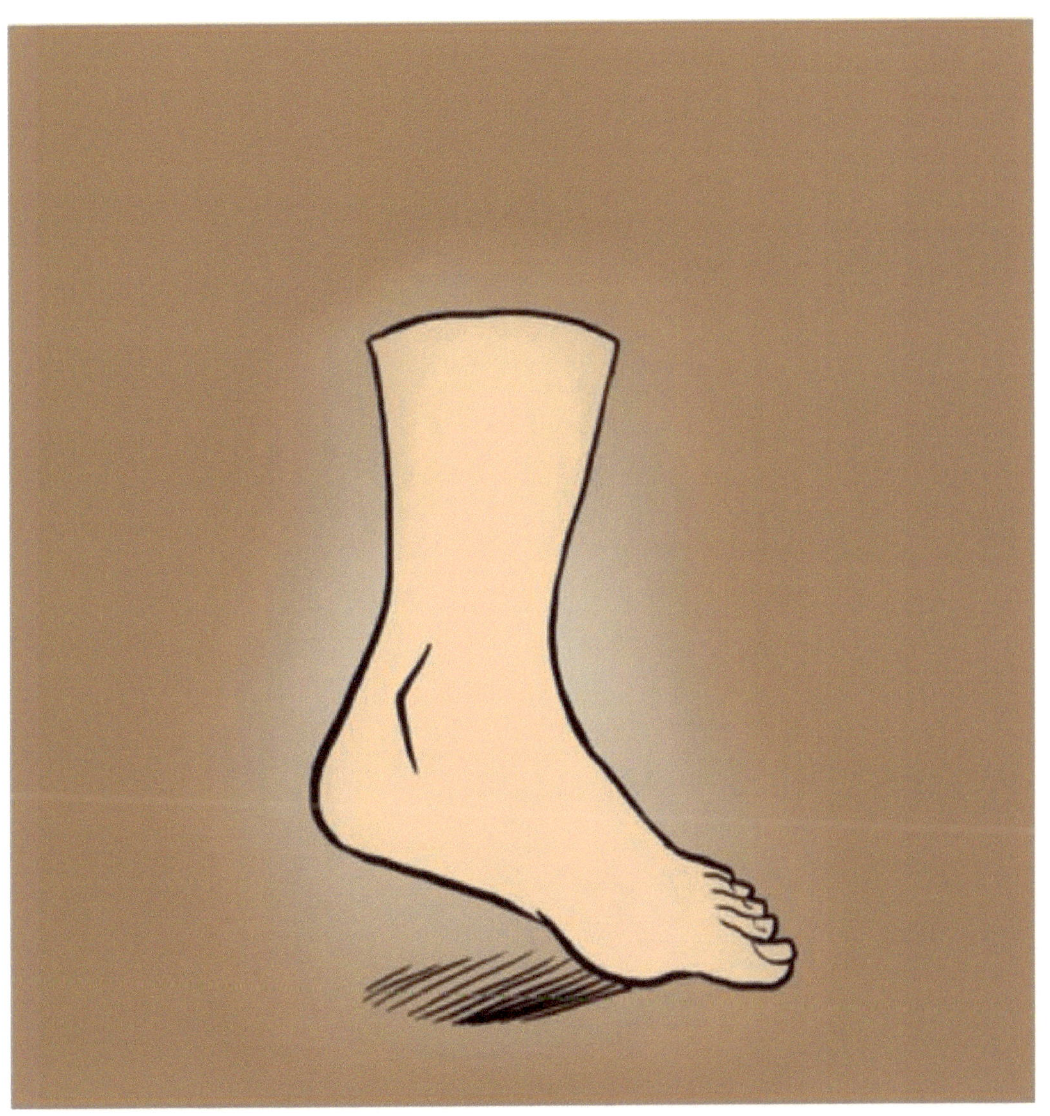

foot

Gg

grass

house

ice

jet

<u>Kk</u>

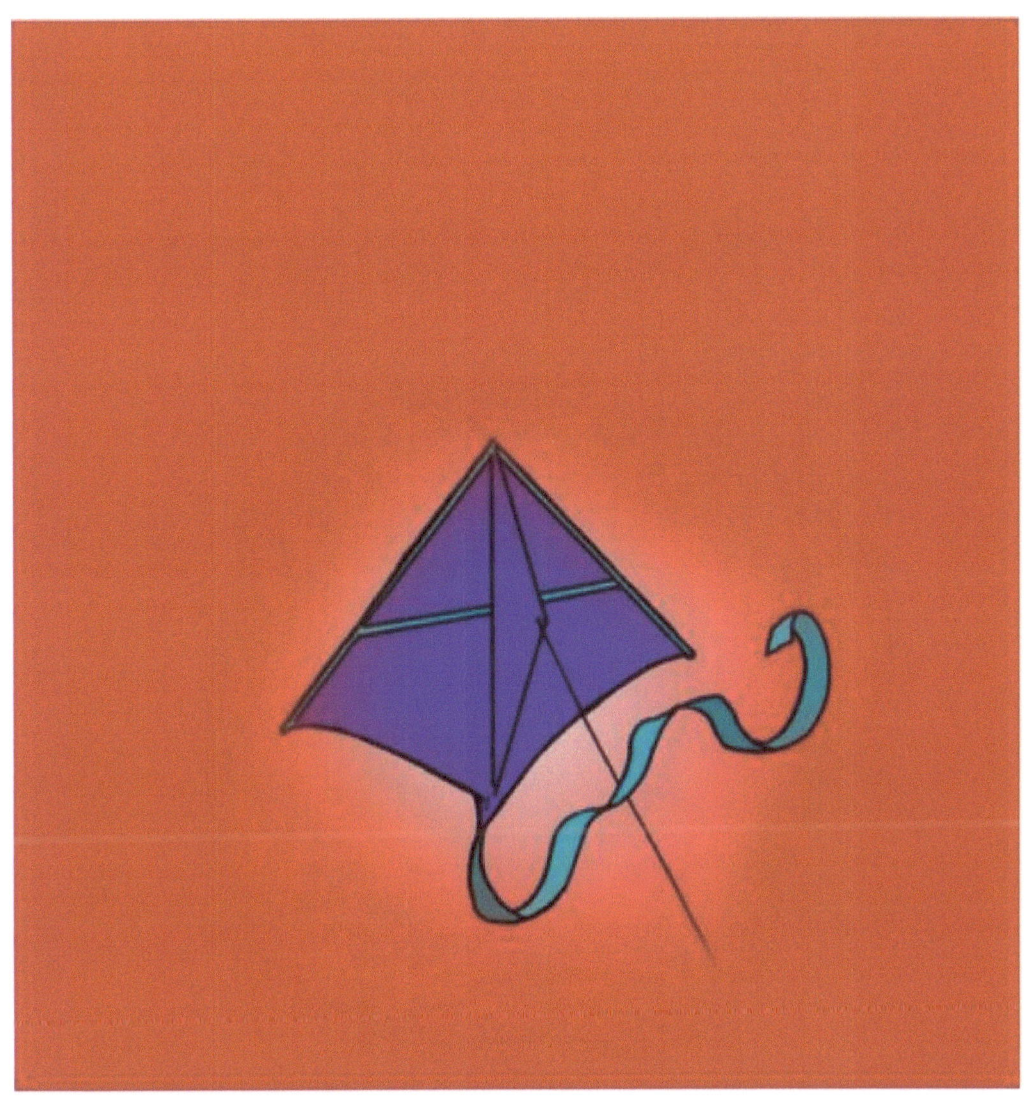

kite

lad

Mm

man

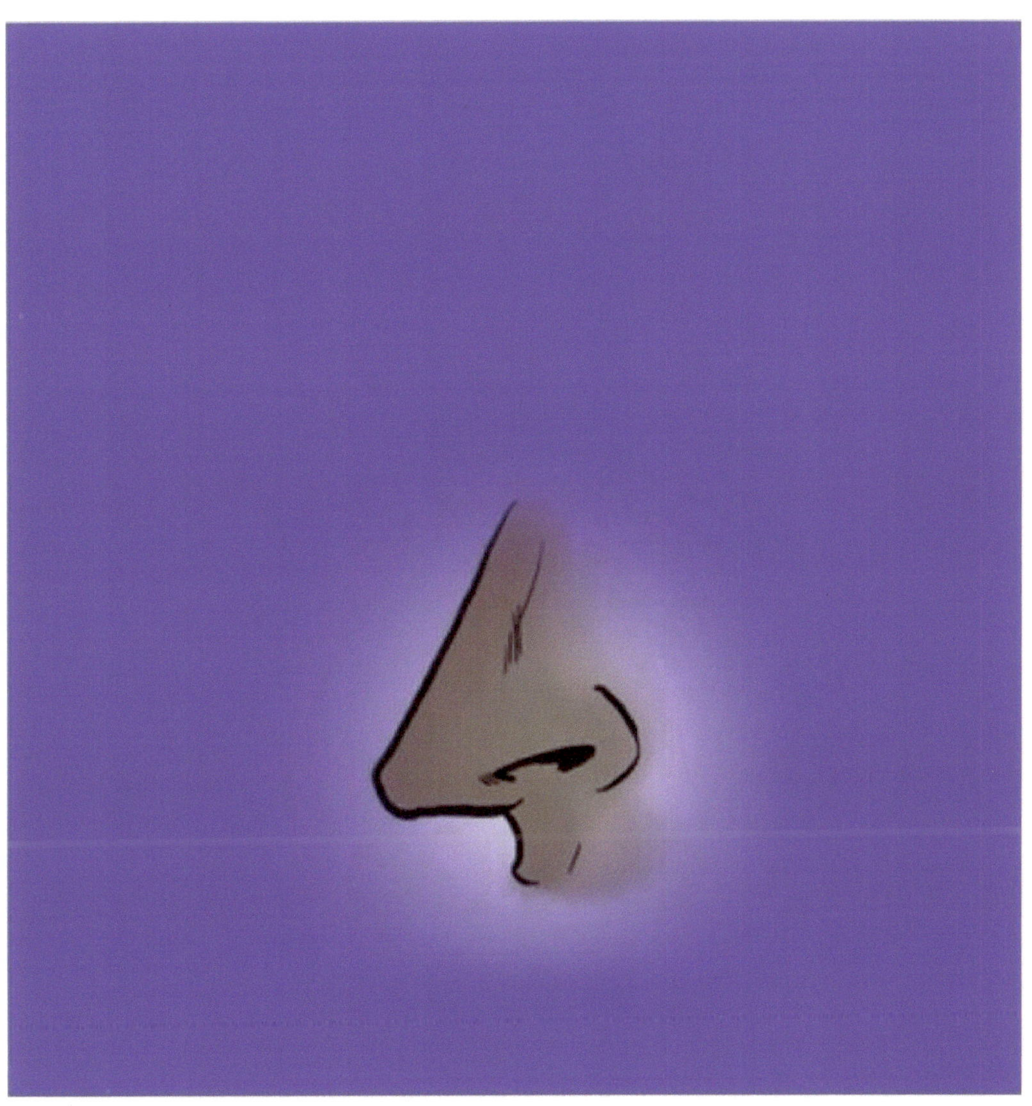

nose

owl

pig

Qq

quail

rat

shoe

tree

Uu

ump

vine

whale

xray

yam

zoo